Christmas Activities

for KS1 Language and Literacy

Irene Yates

Brilliant Publications

Other books in the series

Christmas Activities for KS2 Language and Literacy   ISBN 978 1 903853 67 2

Christmas Activities for KS1 Maths   ISBN 978 1 903853 68 9

Christmas Activities for KS2 Maths   ISBN 978 1 903853 69 6

Published by Brilliant Publications

Sales and despatch:
    BEBC Brilliant Publications
    Albion Close, Parkstone, Poole, Dorset, BH12 3LL
    Tel: 01202 712910
    Fax: 0845 1309300
    email: brilliant@bebc.co.uk
    website:www.brilliantpublications.co.uk

Editorial and marketing:
    Brilliant Publications
    Unit 10, Sparrow Hall Farm, Edlesborough, Dunstable
    Bedfordshire LU6 2ES

The name Brilliant Publications and its logo are registered trademarks.

Written by Irene Yates
Illustrated by Gaynor Berry
Cover design by Z2 Repro
Cover illustration by Chantal Kees

ISBN 978 1 903853 66 5

First published in 2004, reprinted 2008.
10 9 8 7 6 5 4 3 2

Printed in the United Kingdom
© Irene Yates 2004

Contents

Introduction

This book has been designed to take you through the term leading up to Christmas, with the targets of the Key Stage 1 Literacy Strategy autumn term for reception and Years 1 and 2 specifically in mind. The book, as a whole, covers a wide spectrum of these targets whilst providing lots of fun activities all linked to Christmas.

The sheets can be used independently and most ask the child to work in the space provided. There are a few activities which require cutting and sticking. Each task, or activity, has educational rigour, making the work suitable for introducing a topic or reinforcing it. The sheets are not designed as time fillers and should not be used as such. They are meant to become an integral part of the teacher's literacy planning for the first term of the year.

Some of the sheets ask the children to share their reading and their writing with other members of the group and this should be encouraged wherever possible.

The contents page shows the exact literacy target for each page, and gives a brief description of the objective of that target. The book is divided into three sections – Reception, Year One and Year Two – and provides targets for Word, Sentence and Text levels in the order in which they occur in the Literacy document. Using the brief description for each objective you can run down the contents page to find objectives that you may wish to reinforce with any particular children. You can tick off the level references to remind yourself of targets you have worked on. (Note: Christmas patterns on page 9 provides practice with handwriting patterns. It has been placed in the reception chapter, but can be used by all ages.)

Have fun!

Christmas words

Read these words:

Christmas   Happy

baby   new

Mary   mother

star   bright

Kings   three

Draw a picture with these things in it.

Christmas guess the word

Copy the word here.

shepherd _____

lamb _____

angel _____

Copy the word here.

gift _____

manger _____

donkey _____

Draw a picture with these things in it.

Christmas word collection

Copy these Christmas words to make a collection.

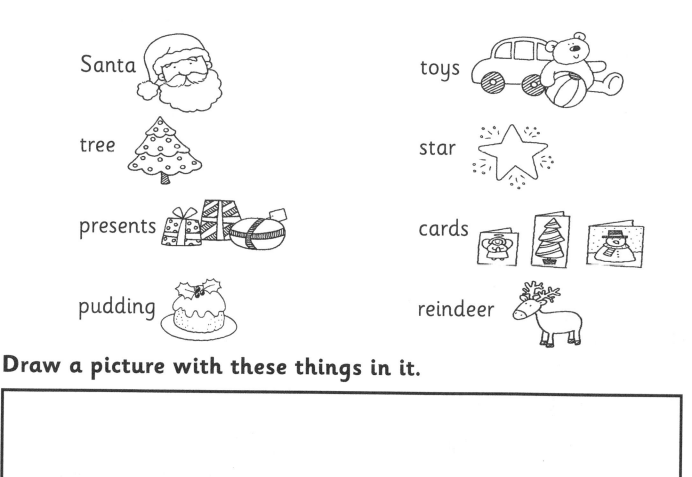

Santa

toys

tree

star

presents

cards

pudding

reindeer

Draw a picture with these things in it.

Can you think of any more Christmas words? Try to write them here.

Handwriting patterns

Continue these patterns.

Copy these patterns.

Can you decorate a card using some of these patterns?

Jesus is born

Fill in the missing words.

Mary and Joseph were on their way __ __
Bethlehem. Mary was going to __ __ __ __
a baby. There was no room __ __ the inn.
They had to sleep __ __ the stable. In the
middle of the night, baby Jesus __ __ __ born.

Write or draw what you think happened next.

The star

Fill in the missing words.

Outside, __ __ the hillside the shepherds woke up.

The angels __ __ __ __ singing. They told the

__ __ __ __ __ __ __ __ __ to follow the star.

Some other people were __ __ __ __ __ __ __ __ __ the star.

They were __ __ __ __ __ wise men who wanted to find

baby __ __ __ __ __. They were carrying __ __ __ __ __

for him.

Where was the star?

Draw a picture of the shepherds and the wise men following the star.

Christmas messages

What are these?

[ ]

[ ]

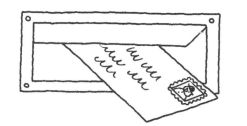

[ ]

[ ]

[ ]

Choose from:
cards
notice
book
newspaper
list
letter

[ ]

Christmas pictogram

Can you read this story?

It was Christmas Eve. In Sophie's house was a

with lots of . At the top was a .

Around the bottom of the tree were lots of .

Sophie was ready for . She knew that

when she was fast asleep would come, riding on

his with his full of toys. She put

a and a on the shelf for Santa and the

reindeer, and off she went to bed.

What would bring her?

Write some more sentences.

Visit to Father Christmas

Read the story:

Mum took Alex to town to see Father Christmas. He was in his grotto. It was very sparkly and there were lots of presents.

Write what Alex said, in his speech bubble.

Letter to Santa

Write a letter to Santa Claus to tell him what you would like for Christmas.

Start 'Dear Santa' and end 'Love from'.

Christmas card

Make a Christmas card for someone you love.

Practise the front here:
What will your picture be?

Choose from:

tree   star

robin   baby Jesus

snowman   king

reindeer   angel

(You may choose more than one.)

Practise the inside here:
What will your message be?

Choose from:
Have a happy Christmas
Merry Christmas
Have lots of fun at Christmas
Christmas is here again
Peace and joy at Christmas

Don't forget to add who the card is to, and who it is from.

Capital letter candles

The Christmas tree has 52 candles on it. 26 have a small letter.
26 are blank.

Write one capital letter for each small letter of the alphabet, in the blank candles.

Cross off the letters you have done.

A B C D E F G H I J K L M N O P Q R S T U V W X Y Z

Snowman's scarf

Poor Snowman! He's very cold.
He needs a scarf and gloves and a hat.

**Finish the patterns on his things so
that he can wear them.**

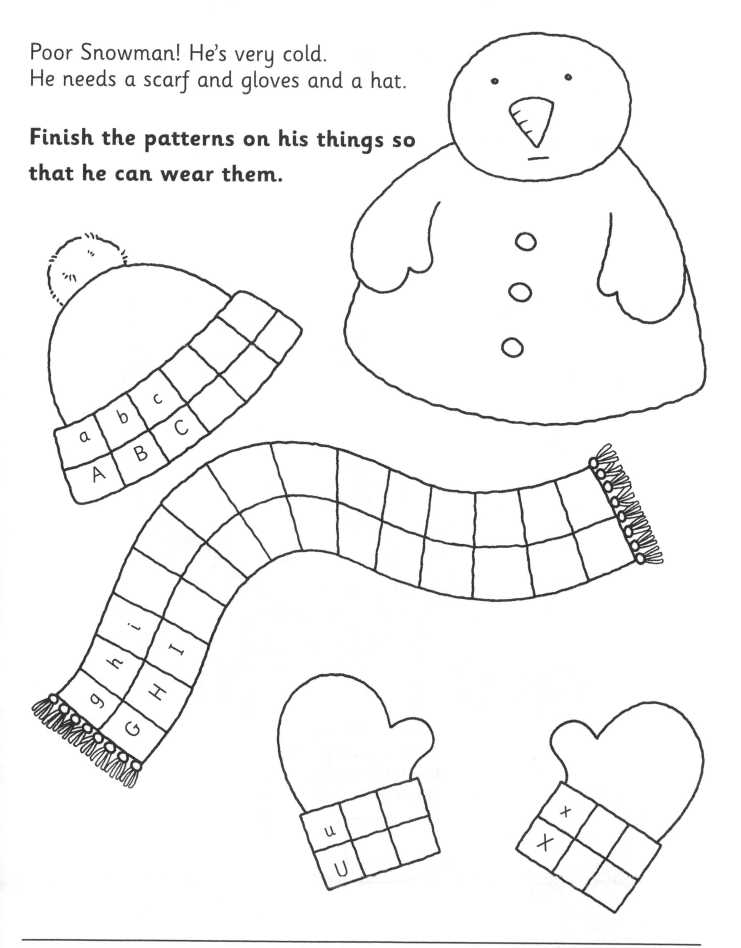

a b c
A B C

g h i
G H I

u
U

x
X

Mr Robin's round-up

While Mr Robin pecks away at the berries, he is practising all the words he can read. Can you help him?

Draw a red berry next to every word he gets right.

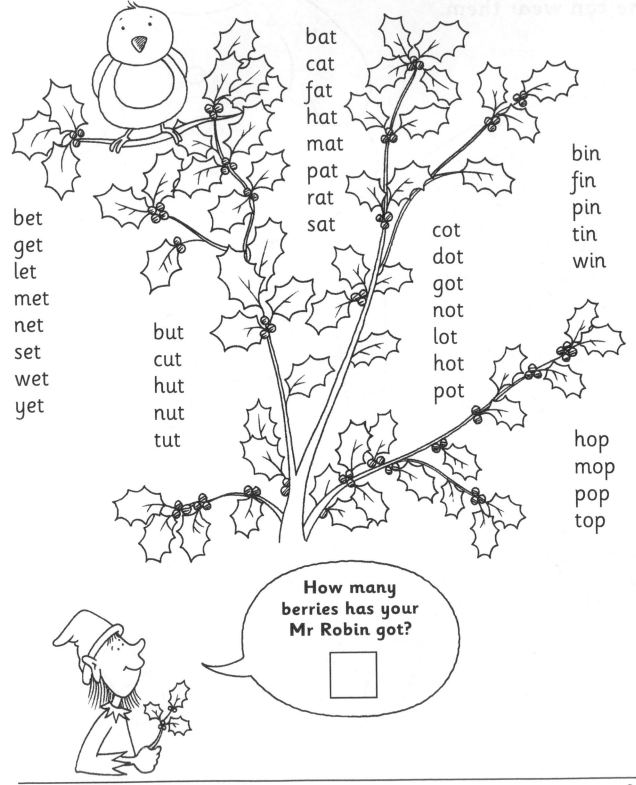

bat
cat
fat
hat
mat
pat
rat
sat

bin
fin
pin
tin
win

bet
get
let
met
net
set
wet
yet

but
cut
hut
nut
tut

cot
dot
got
not
lot
hot
pot

hop
mop
pop
top

How many berries has your Mr Robin got?

Christmas crackers

Each Christmas cracker has a word inside it. Read the word to colour in the cracker.

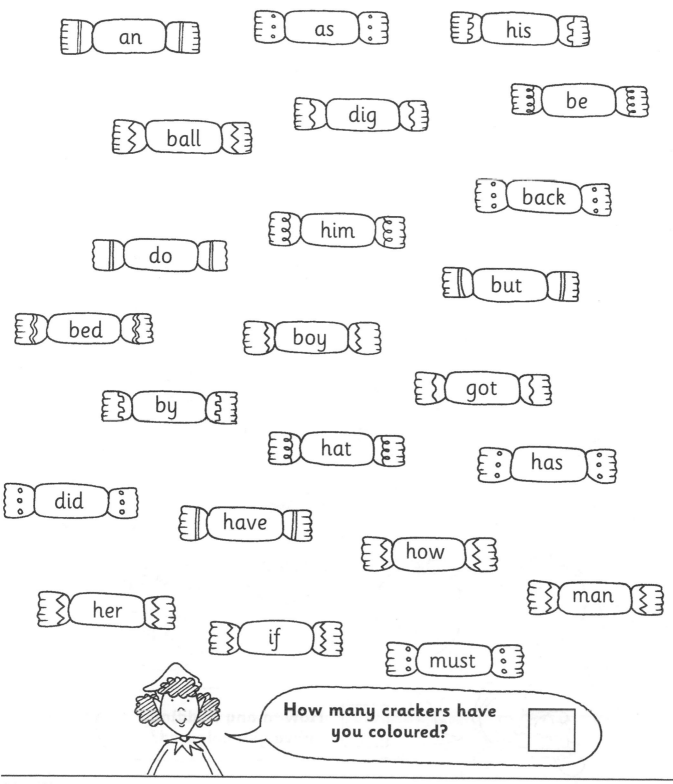

an

as

his

dig

be

ball

back

him

do

but

bed

boy

got

by

hat

has

did

have

how

her

if

man

must

How many crackers have you coloured?

Christmas Activities for KS1 Language and Literacy

Christmas puddings

Each Christmas pudding has a word in it.
Read the word to colour the pudding.

our

not

off

one

ran

pull

or

put

saw

than

by

so

that

there

three

tree

with

will

us

what

want

your

when

How many puddings have you coloured?

Make a Christmas word book

Take a sheet of paper.

Fold it into four.

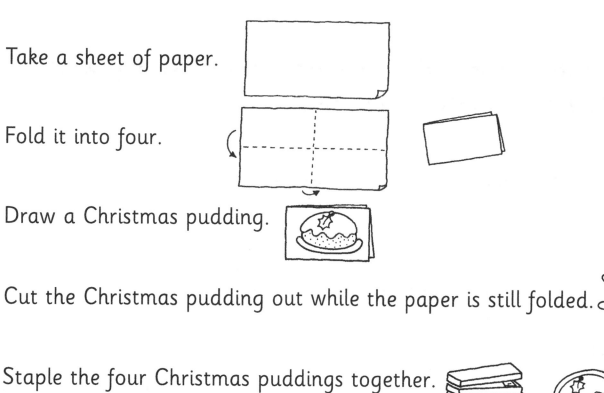

Draw a Christmas pudding.

Cut the Christmas pudding out while the paper is still folded.

Staple the four Christmas puddings together.

Write 'My Christmas Words' on the front.

Here are some words to write in your book:

pudding
presents
cards
carols
holly
robin
snowman
tree

baby
Mary
Joseph
donkey
King
shepherd
angel
inn

Can you put your words in alphabetical order?

Can you think of some more words?

Christmas time

Read this story. Some of it does not make sense. Put a circle round the bits you think are wrong.

At Christmas time, everyone has a holiday. The children don't go to school for two weeks. They stay up home and help to got everything ready on Christmas.

Most people put down a tree. They decorate it with lights to make it sparkles. At the top it put a star or a fairy. Underneath, they have lots for presents.

The children wait to Santa to come. He always brings toy so they liked him very much.

Write another sentence, without any mistakes.

Santa sentences

Write a sentence to go with each picture.

Read it back to make sure it makes sense.

Santa is loading the sleigh.

Christmas Activities for KS1 Language and Literacy

Starry, starry night

Look at the pictures. Write a caption for each picture.
The first one is done, to show you how.

Journey to Bethlehem

Santa's sack

Which are sentences?
Write the sentences in Santa's sack.

Christmas is a fun time.

lots of fun

lots of presents

We decorate the tree.

star on top

This is my present list.

turkey for dinner

candles to light

We light all the candles.

Have a happy Christmas.

carrot and mince pie and stocking

Can you come to my Christmas party?

How do you know something is a sentence?

Christmas windows

Read these instructions with a friend.

Make a Christmas window each.

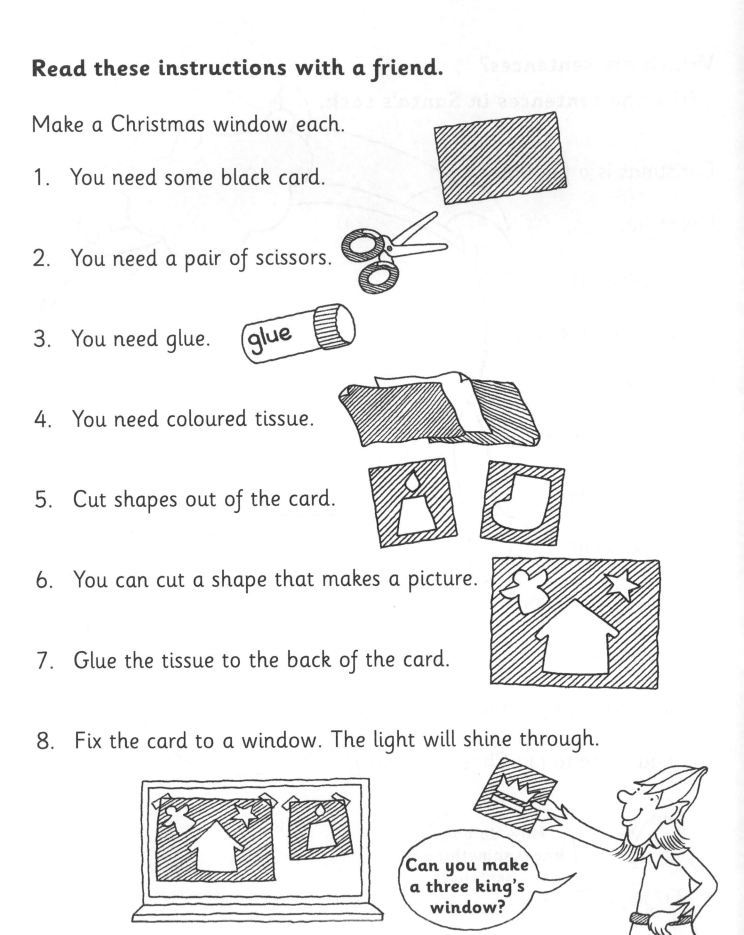

1. You need some black card.

2. You need a pair of scissors.

3. You need glue.

4. You need coloured tissue.

5. Cut shapes out of the card.

6. You can cut a shape that makes a picture.

7. Glue the tissue to the back of the card.

8. Fix the card to a window. The light will shine through.

Can you make a three king's window?

Christmas story

Think about last Christmas.

Write a story telling what happened to you.

My Christmas

Nativity story book

Make a nativity story book.

You need two pieces of paper.
Fold them in half.
Staple them together.

On the front, write the title and
your name.
Number the pages, 1 to 6.

Colour and cut out the pictures at the bottom of the sheet.
Stick a picture on each page.
Write some sentences for each page.

Read your book with a friend.
Read your friend's book as well.

The nativity
by
Jack Archer

Make sure
they're in the
right order!

Christmas decorations

Make some paper chains.

You need coloured paper.

You need scissors.

You need glue.

Cut the paper into thin strips.

Curl one strip round to make a ring.

Glue the ends.

Put another strip through the ring.

Glue the ends.

Put another strip through that ring.

Glue the ends.

Keep going until you have a long paper chain.

Hang it up.

What colours will you use?

Christmas card list

Make a list of all the people you want to send
a Christmas card to.

How many people are
on your list?

Making candles

Write instructions for
making a paper candle:

1

2

3

4

5

6

7

Have you
made a candle?

Busy elves

Can you put these words into the right sacks for the elves?
Read the words first.

feet
train
wheat
day
pie
meet
say
rain
my
cry
street
meat
dry
chain
brain
sheet
stay
pain
beat
pay
by
tie
seat
fly
play

More busy elves

Can you put these words into the right sacks for the elves? Read the words first.

boat
blow
rode
pole
woke
moon
coat
few
low
true
snow
chew
mole
new
moan
spoon
goat
rope
grow
hope
slow
blue
note
toad
hole

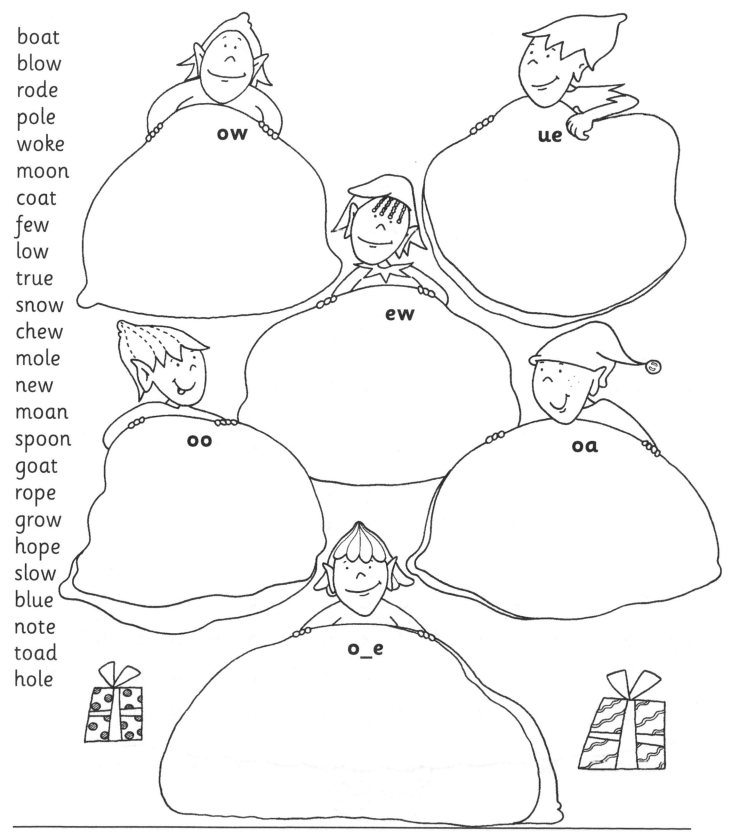

ow

ue

ew

oo

oa

o_e

Christmas Activities for KS1 Language and Literacy

Christmas tree wordsearch

The elves have learned four new vowel sounds. Say the sounds.

Look for these words on the Christmas tree:

good	star	boy	how
hood	bar	joy	cow
stood	car	toy	now
wood	far	wow	bow

Colour in each word you find.

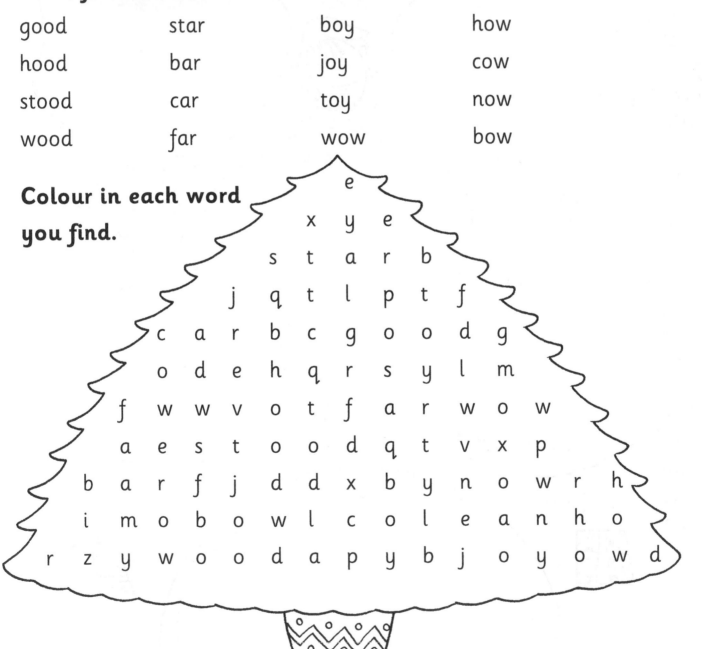

Christmas tree baubles

Each bauble has a word inside it.
Read the word to decorate the bauble.

again

been

about

after

another

because

can't

brother

called

came

could

from

lived

laugh

don't

here

many

little

home

house

may

down

how

much

more

just

first

could

How many baubles have you decorated?

Christmas tree lights

Each light has a word inside it.
Read the word to decorate the light.

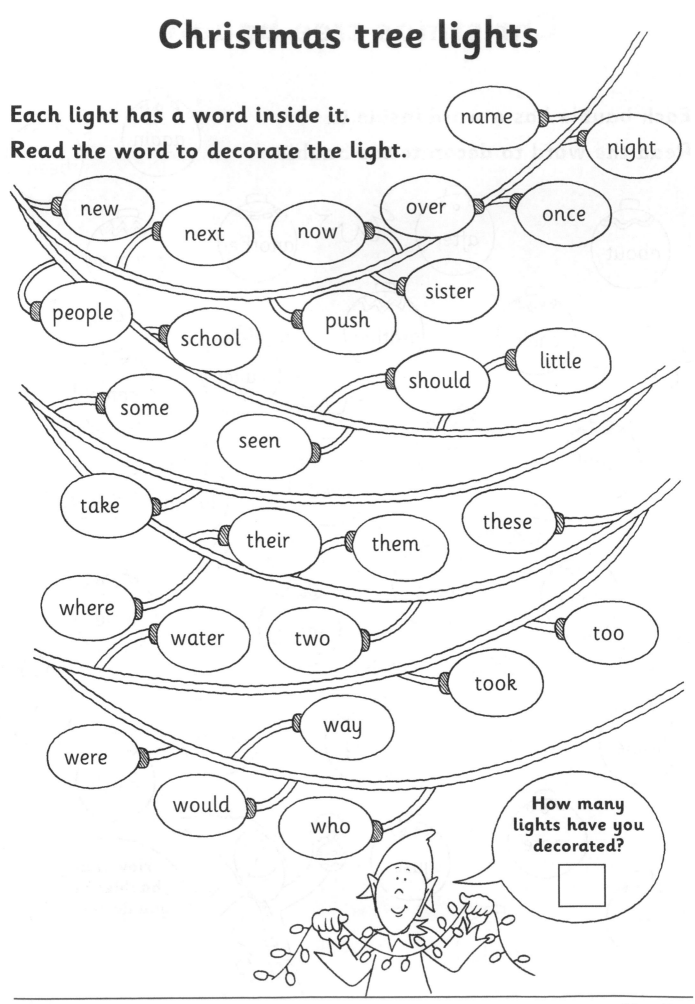

name

night

new

next

now

over

once

people

school

push

sister

some

seen

should

little

take

their

them

these

where

water

two

too

took

were

way

would

who

How many lights have you decorated?

Nativity

Add the vowels to complete the nativity scene:

st__r

T__ y__ __
th__s d__y __
ch__ld __s
b__rn

__ng__l s__ng__ng

b__by
J__s__s

m__ng__r

M__ry

J__s__ph

sh__ph__rds w__th l__mbs

Can you tell the story?

thr__ __ k__ngs w__th g__fts

Remember, the vowels are
a e i o u

Make a Christmas mobile

Can you fill in the missing words?

You can _____ a Christmas mobile. It _____ very easy.

First, you _____ two strips _____ card.

Cut a slit in the middle of _____ strip.

Dab some glue _____ each slit.

Slot them _____ to make a cross.

Use some old Christmas _____.

Cut _____ pictures.

Use a needle to thread them _____ cotton.

Thread the cotton through the cross and _____ them carefully.

They _____ need to balance.

Hang _____ mobile up.

Can you make the mobile?

What I really want

What would you really like for Christmas? Pretend you could have anything in the whole world that you would like.

Write about it here.

Did you make any mistakes? Have another go!

Read it back to make sure:

* it makes sense
* you have spelled all the words correctly
* you have used capital letters and full stops properly.

Present mix-up

Santa's elves have got lots of presents to load, but all the labels are wrong. Someone has not thought about capital letters! Could you write the labels on them properly?

Your should always use a capital letter for a name.

Whoops! I forgot!

These are the names:
sam
ben
ellie
ranjit
sophie
imrah
jason
clare
kirandip
lizzie
daniel
tracey

Where else should you use a capital letter?

Back at the workshop

Read this story. Fill in the missing words.

There are clues at the bottom of the page to help you.

It was Christmas _____ at the workshop. Everyone was busy, helping to tidy up. Santa and the reindeer had gone off on their _____. The _____ was loaded with toys. There was a full sack to go down every _____ in the land. It was a beautiful, _____ night and the elves felt very _____.

When Santa came back they would have a big _____. There would be _____ for everyone, lots of _____ and a huge _____.

'Merry Christmas!' they all called to each other.

Clues:

We go on this to get to a different place

_ _ _ _ _ _ _

The day before Christmas day   _ _ _

It's on the roof   _ _ _ _ _ _ _

The sky is lit up   _ _ _ _ _ _

We do this when music plays   _ _ _ _ _ _ _

The reindeer pull it   _ _ _ _ _

We give these to each other   _ _ _ _ _ _ _ _

Full of good cheer   _ _ _ _ _ _ _

We have one of these on special days   _ _ _ _ _ _ _ _ _ _ _ _

A huge meal   _ _ _ _ _

The clues are not in the right order!

That would be too easy!

Christmas morning

Talk about these pictures with a friend. What's happening in them?
What happens in your house on Christmas morning?

Draw a set of pictures and write a sentence for each one.

Share your pictures and
sentences with a friend.

Last Christmas

Read this story:

Last Christmas, at school, Tom was Joseph in the nativity play. His mum made him a costume out of an old T-shirt. He had a teatowel for his headdress, with some special string round it.

Tom practised his words every night. He wanted to do his best because his grandad was coming to watch him.

On the afternoon of the play, everyone was there. Tom did his part so well that everybody clapped.

Didn't he feel proud!

What do you remember about last Christmas at school?

Write a story about it, like this story.

Christmas poem

Read the poem, then write two new verses of your own.
Make them fit the same pattern.

Here comes Christmas!
Here comes Christmas!
Happy day!
Happy day!
Lots of lovely presents,
Lots of lovely presents,
Shout, 'Hurray!'
Shout, 'Hurray!'

Here comes Santa! _____

_____

_____

_____

_____

_____

Here comes _____

_____

_____

_____

_____

_____

Say or
sing your poem
with a group of
friends.

Make a Father Christmas

Write the instructions:

Think about how
to set out your
instructions.

Have you made the
Father Christmas?

Design your own stationery

Here is an idea for making Christmas stationery. Unfortunately, the instructions are in the wrong order. Write them out again in the order they should be.

Write the instructions here in the right order.

Cut round them in a circle or any shape you like.

Choose some wrapping paper.

Stick a picture, or pictures, to the card.

Make a card.

Make a label in the same way.

Cut out lots of the pictures.

Choose just one picture to repeat, or different ones.

Use more than one picture to make a pattern on another card or label.

1

2

3

4

5

6

7

8

Christmas potato prints

The elves have made a set of instructions for printing with potatoes, but they forgot to draw the diagrams.

Draw the diagrams to go with the instructions.

1. Clean a potato.

2. Cut it in half.

3. Cut a Christmas design on it.

4. Put paint in a flat dish.

5. Dip the potato into the paint.

6. Press the design on to the paper.

7. Use two halves of potato to do two colours.

Don't forget to label your diagrams.

I made a green holly leaf print.

Have fun!

Answers

Jesus is born (page 9)
to; have; at; in; was

The star (page 10)
on; were; shepherds; following; three; Jesus;
gifts

The star was over the stable.

Christmas pictogram (page 12)
Christmas tree; decorations (baubles); star;
presents (gifts); bed; Santa; sleigh; sack;
mince pie; carrot; Santa

Christmas time (page 22)
Grammatical errors:
up – at; got – get; on – for; down – up;
sparkles – sparkle; it – they; for – of; to – for;
toy – toys; liked – like

Santa's sack (page 25)
The following are sentences:
Christmas is a fun time.
We decorate the tree.
This is my present list.
We light all the candles.
Have a happy Christmas.
Can you come to my Christmas party?

Busy elves (page 32)
ee – feet; meet; street; sheet
ea – wheat; meat; beat, seat
ai – train; rain; chain; brain; pain
ay – day; say; stay; pay; play
y – my; cry; dry; by; fly
ie – pie; tie

More busy elves (page 33)
oa – boat; coat; moan; goat; toad
ow – blow; low; snow; grow; slow
o_e – rode; pole; woke; mole: rope; hope;
note; hole
oo – moon; spoon
ew – few; chew; new
ue – true; blue

Christmas tree wordsearch (page 34)

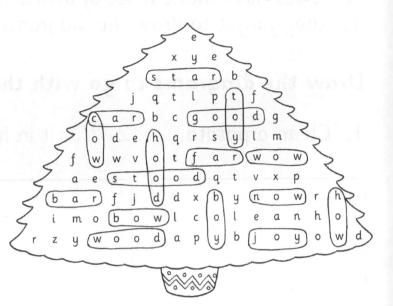

Nativity (page 37)
star; To you this day a child is born; angel
singing; baby Jesus; manger; Mary;
Joseph; shepherds with lambs; three kings
with gifts

Make a Christmas mobile (page 38)
make; is; need (take); of; each; on;
together; cards; out; with; tie; will; your

Back at the workshop (page 41)
Eve; journey; sleigh; chimney; starry;
cheerful; celebration; presents; dancing;
feast

Design your own stationery (page 46)
Choose some wrapping paper.
Cut out lots of the pictures.
Cut round them in a circle or any shape you
like.
Choose just one picture to repeat, or
different ones.
Make a card.
Stick a picture, or pictures, to the card.
Make a label in the same way.
Use more than one picture to make a
pattern on another card or label.

Lightning Source UK Ltd.
Milton Keynes UK
UKOW06f0647221113

221597UK00002B/18/P